WARSAW *BIKINI*

WARSAW

BIKINI

SANDRA SIMONDS

To Hillary
Thanks for coming!
Thank you!
S

BLOOF 🐝 **BOOKS**

Published by Bloof Books
www.bloofbooks.com
Central New Jersey

Bloof Books are distributed to the trade via Ingram and other wholesalers
in the US, Bertrams and Gardners in the UK, or directly from the press.
Individuals may purchase them from our website, from online retailers
such as Powells.com and Amazon.com, or request them from their favorite
bookstores. (Please support your local independent bookseller whenever
possible.)

ISBN: 978-0-615-25623-8

To my mother and father, sister and husband.

MY RED BIKE DING DONG

HULLABALOO FLOWERS

STEAM

NOTES
ACKNOWLEDGMENTS
ABOUT THE AUTHOR

MY RED BIKE DING DONG

I SERENGETI YOU

like a banshee, a leprechaun, a geek
in the shuffling feet of trick neurons
limbic, I skipped
town with your checkbook
rode limber sleuths through suburban felts on the flushed cheek,
from gill to aorta, renal to fallopian tube
twirling like Mendel's string bean.

In the covered wagon of the corpus collosum
traveled to Coca Island, my mind's coliseum
sliding off your mansion's
cedar banister wowed superstellar monks a high-altitude kiss
where the prevailing winds
clipped their yak-butter-colored robes.

As long as I could
through white matter grids, pons, gas plants, ice plants, gum
trees, steam
pouring from a half-inch medulla hole

Eating gumbo on a glacier of
you melt my global warming

Peeling squash by a saguaro of
you alkaline my pesticides

Doing jumping jacks on Mount Rushmore,
slurping udon noodles
my brothy stomach bulimic, bubonic,
influenzic, tubercular, emptying out
a department store's clearance rack
—gaunt mannequin of me, *oh where oh where
can my Gucci be?*

Well-dressed and indefatigable in my aquamarine goggles
on this timetable highway of cranial nerves
where a brute Genghis Kahn aphasia transfixes
me forward—One June day I promise to rescue
baby Jessica trapped
in her pipe, repair the Challenger's
tummy of cosmonauts   busted open
through an ozone   hole the size
of sixteen Oklahomas   but for now

Doctor Dura Mater, so skull to meet you
wear your you so well   please put
your stethoscope to coal my syndrome chest
and tell me
where to asphyxiate
the piranha, the red-eyed firefly,
kinkajou and newt—
because the Amazon's a
goner, a game show's gong.

I have an endowed chair at Dogbonne University.
    Other than that, the future
of academia looks bleak teaching historic jazz quartets
    to a fuzz of locked bleach blondes
    chain-ganged to iPods. My colleague
wears a chiffon hummingbird on dress-down Wednesdays
    much to the chagrin of our
admired chair. Favorite quote?
The only way to pick a lock is with a rib eye steak—
                Alexis de Tocqueville (1832)

Try to be a nonconformist, I advised Anna-Marie.
        We spent quality time at an excavation site
    in Chattahoochee where
our team of experts unearthed the frontier: how to build
    miniature Scotch-Irish coffins with the basics—tooth-
        picks and graham crackers.

    Our motto was…*with antisocial behaviors so sophisticated, with*
        such a passion for bayonets, such exquisite marks-
manship, how could anyone not be seduced by these hit-
and-run guerrillas, rucksack clad
        itinerant laborers, tribes of hash? Should have known
      she'd fuck any trash
        that moved her polyurethane
          leg to replace the one she lost
          in a skiing accident
            near Place des Vosges.

    Yes, we went on field trips. Yes to all questions!

Do I know everything about humpback whales?

Does the blitzkrieg affect primogeniture in Palestine?

Isn't urea thermal insulation around instrument bezels?

Did you buy that body armor in Manhattan?

Do you think Colorado history is as crass as a 49-dollar gold rush egg?

Is *Marianne* a spaghetti western?

I want to move to Paris,
to listen to Tchaikovsky, make oil
        paintings of the Ebola virus, want to know
        why she's hobbled off
        with a rich and well-born
                plankton researcher, an Asst. Prof. at Dogbonne,
                who seeks to protect
                        the minority of the opulent
                                from endless scrolls of Dead Sea tax bills.

THE TRUTH ABOUT THE PILLS I TOOK

color me the spiral siren against an august sweatshop
for the forehead of the immigrant's wet face
me when you speak and don't fidget

bitter its molecular structures
         dire the way he holds me to his tire chest—or the donut curved
blood cell is saturated   with a pollen wild

as in these pastel feathers   the yellow jacket nerves
fray and not too painfully yours   is the one we will call "asphyxia
at dusk" when the dusk hawk stares the ocean down into pull me undertow

but you are more exhausted   than the simple lack of sleep
     and all my one sixteenths of truth stick to my hemoglobin mouth
          so when the wrought iron
gate
opens
the flesh field—the story
goes as follows...[once upon a midnight we lived on...Mount...Up...There...
snow freeze in the nostrils—the aryan climate of deer,
     pine needles   and forget-me-nots dunked into steam soup

I can see you logarithmically
ascending
the staircase
of it's so homey and warm here
in order to
               dump those little fractions of sound
 into the toilet   the morse code I've been studying what it's like to be
lost at sea
          pitter pat that diagonal weather
you must steady the hawk gaze   the false
flush of the face   land-ho in the map palm
          and now I live where the weather never dips below a cold sweat
     where the sewing machines tap tap tap
                    must *steady the white flag hands*

THESE DAYS ARE MALTHUSIAN FOOTNOTES

Like a bildungsroman at the center of a pile
of Warsaw war snow
beating like uncle wound
or the cuckoo clock's beak's
scheduled meeting with o'clock,

one wing of the bird was left for me. That the animal eats, shits

and dies free.

Oh to be like Dutch painter X in the honeydew
light of March flanked by three golden retrievers,

rot iron pots and pans, or to be somewhat quartz / somewhat syrup

on Florida's one hundred and one degrees

in cocktails and jazz.

She wades in a pool of serum and amoebas where the oil slick
is a speech act that is duct taped over the ear
syllable by sound.

And where is the snow, Warsaw?
The zero's blank corpse sounds over crops   erotic as gas
and the asbestos that tang the lungs into submission tumors, into blue trees—
(you're a tame dog) but they are not ze-
ro, Romeo,
they are not know-
ing.

ODE TO THE ADVENTURE WRITER

I carry sixteen passports and know eight languages
just like Sallah in
Indiana Jones and the Last Crusade
who sticks his thumb into a Peruvian pan flute and
emerges from the airliner as
postmodern as Giovanni Versace, who,
even though killed by a serial killer
remains permanently scarred by his
sister's overtanned face and *really bad hair.*
Throwing a date

into the air and waiting for the spider monkey
to catch it with his diminutive hand
is the least of your problems. Besides, that might
not even be the movie and you're the best
actress they've got for the sequel up until now.
So, put that Eddie Bauer garb on and get out there!
You've got your assignments on who the
King of the Crocs *really was* and what went wrong
at the Coca-Cola plant in Western Siberia.

It's tough to be shoved off your own
narrative. When the writer deems you unworthy of
your wildest dreams involve dung beetles
and wildebeests, there's a certain *je ne sais quoi*
about the revolving doors of an agricultural revolution
finds young Indy permanently convulsing
on the set, microphone between male breasts.

We need his double. Get her quick.
Just a bit before that grunge hit song on the tip of
the boom-cha-cha-boom Viper Room's tongue.

THE PHYSIOLOGICAL INFESTATION OF THE LEAP THAT LOOKS BACK

You had an ink-
ling the "there"
would be trouble. Cur-
tain call. The actor
jabs a fork into an onstage outlet.
A cadaver of caviar: *quelle*
voltage.

The audience is a water-
color mural that told me
if you cut into any body
you'll find fish
eggs. Their belladonna
eyes swim in pigment, mad
as sperm up fallopian
tubes. The actor

tells us one
thing, and one thing only, lying
there. There's

a place in the body as
beautiful as an
aquarium and even if you touch it, even if
you put your two lips to it,
romance language it along its glass

curves or fuck it until
it shivers, still
you cannot feel it—
lying there, un-
known.

PARABLE THAT TAKES PLACE IN LITTLE NATHANIEL'S CLOSET

Just when you throw up
your hands

and say "I'm really a horrible
person," there's an-

other selfsame self that
assures you you are in-

deed more horrible
than previously suspected.

How dis-
proportionate!

It follows, then, that hidden
in this haunted mansion

a nuisance ghost
dressed up as grandpapa

pecks out your sleep and just
when you recognize that it's you

this you has re-
ceded into the cedar splintered

closet of the flesh saying—
"you see you're worse than me."

SALT LATITUDES

white rose of island   gallops as my burglar thumps drawers
ich this midnight unto the burlap skin of   palmtree /on/ palmtree

       footfalls's woolen   anxieties triangulate their own cutouts
to werewolves&wherewithals   climate shorn hisses

           iris the ich, your smirk is the rubber band bones that
fizzle like vinegar   and soda pop

anything can quench diamonds   you said   as in exotic footage of orangutans
and eclipses or orange-peel candies as puritanical as
sugar lack afrique and citric acid   —this here
not the   drawer

      rose white in pallor
       it stung   a primate   in her burglary itch her withins mock

so sunny   dank spoke your doorstep in lavender climates   a
coconut glistened
on
  a
   common palm

       in a season of water   she sank   so stolen   like a heavy
coin off a plank
         gaze in the gauze   dress of rinsing

the getaway and   come hither ties   —not the closet

    for an archipelago of rock salt   isles of ich and il y a

gentleman of ocean wrapped sleep,   my somewhat guarantees in a stam-

pede   of believe. you. me. she was   a screendoor for wasps

the last calf out the window
zeitgeist in the oh's pickpocket

I AM SMALL

but my life is enormous. Huge
as angels. Huge as a zookeeper's

heart. Who knows
how large this zoo is

when you take into account all
the cages—arterial strings, penises

nipples, sweat glands, furs, aortas, pins.
Let's get hitched in the roomy cage of

the latest newly extinct
species. He's

gone. There's room.
In this country they make lists (in

hieroglyphics) of all the unions
that have ever taken place

and all the unions that
will ever take place.

There's no way out of this one, Sam.

That's what they call a "nation."
That's when they ask the syringe

and turkey baster
holding zookeeper

to sedate
the African elephants

and artificially inseminate the black
and white, blasé pandas.

KNAPSACK OF RITZ CRACKERS

Simonds: you boo-hoo Jew who
steps through a sky of blue tumors,
enters Forest Wayward in wild cells, whooping
cough birds, wildebeests and the wolf's riding hood gulp.

Where is your wicker basket with the
fresh Washington apples
of his sooty eyes? Don't throw
a fit like sperm 6743's whipping tail!
Kick around your "plus
the pupil," inward whoosh, (the better
to), of tunnel, kick around your minus stones
that stub the toes to real Cunning
and wheeze the lungs with Not Dare You My
Derring-do & when you're through cleave

me from these dis-
interested third parties.
Granny gather eggs with the blood cups
—sockets—doth you protest—
and in your tra-la-la September not a
crimson dress to tear away
the skinned, frozen knot you step
through half the throatless hoop

A POEM FOR DAVID SCHUBERT

Went to the valley and it was green went to the valley
    red to the vineyard and found the grapes went to the vineyard

why don't you thank your fortune why don't you let down your hair?
    Walked the road, snake-shaped road walked to the doorstep for water.

May I have some water, good doorstep, may I have my friend has left
    me for a cold cup of water for a cold cup of water he why

don't you write your name on my doorstep when the sun is the sun again?
    Winter came and he was no longer a friendship why not write down your

went to the valley to the clear-cold valley when the sun was the sun he says
    a stranger is the gift of water and his grey eyes are the only ones to believe.

Stranger, may I have your hand or a mirror, dear, may I have a word
    of advice? Went to the valley and it was a red went to the valley white.

A long-legged deer stood by the roadside and drank his crystal waters.
    May I have your soft step or a mirror, deer, may I have a word of advice?

Come sit by the waters and feel the breeze and let down your hair, my dear,
Write your name on my doorstep write your name on this roadside
                            for the sun is the sun again.

BON VOYAGE

The path from the throat
to the nipple is too long

a journey to take without
handkerchief and water

so goodbye
bulky red

train—pulse sack of meat,
metal and nail

because my flesh is an artificial
field of feel where each cell

is a different
explanation, each nook

an anxiety to quell
and hello,

again, rail-thin
destination, hello you

somewhat soul,
you ticktock

conductor, you black funnel—
pupilful

of the choo-choo's
red soot.

HULLABALOO FLOWERS

I DON'T DESERVE YOUR RIESLING

My architect builds my love from scratch
    and he uses a defibrillator
when the pharmacist urges *only ipecac.*

  He patents the enzymes of my tachycardia
    and my two lungs are twice the fluffy
bunny slippers of his jet stream robotics.

  A fire ant crawls from my pupil
    to a femur-sized fruit bowl of fermenting
bananas and I piss lemonade every day
so that the sky will sing to me.

Of my *knock-knock* knees
    he uses three mints that spark a
who's there brushfire—

  a telephone's crosswired correspondence:
yes, that's the webbing of feet
    sewed to the face of an oakless metropolis.

  I'm more like a cast for wrists that melt
    when melting is good for your eardrums
than the Louvre that houses
      thirty-five thousand works of art.

  You can punch a nostril in the pleather trampoline
    of my navel and a few bits of gravel will fall
to the floorboards—maybe a pigeon if you're lucky.

My architect builds my love from scratch.
    He puts a teaspoon of baking soda on my tongue and
teaches me an exercise to turn it into a stone.

When he is done he sends me my cardiogram,
    a CD of love songs soaked in iodine and an invoice
with a post-it note that says
    you may never amount to anything.

WRITING MY BIKE IN CIRCLES AROUND THIS POEM
TO PROVE THAT I PERSIST

I'm not settling like a formaldehyde drizzle on the morgue sea
of looping and looping figure eights
where junk DNA   births frozen snakes
and the Styrofoam moon pulls   pill-shaped lesions
out of a grey matter nightjar from which the dolphins dart so

be my Psychopomp, my amnesia egg where break's
a feathered static the sound of a green balloon
going crazy losing air
to good-willed mouth-to-mouth resuscitators.

My 4th mug shot grows claws, Psychopomp.
It grows a twelve-inch tail of itch that looks
like a dependent clause twenty-three politicians long
swatting horseflies. I have hooves
of sugar and huff on fog and
they say I'm tough on crime but really
(as my 2nd photo proves) I'm just
the mouthpiece that keeps the poem agog.

Where the double-jointed hermaphrodite on the shoreline
turns its white ruffled dress into a ladle for the tide,
I'm the saltwater dispatch, a slab of sand
in the image of *George Washington Crossing the Delaware,* a face
ferociously like yours.

Psychopomp, I've revised myself into being's anon and anon
I'm riding my red bike ding dong
straight into the water, past the minotaur and the hermaphrodite
the EMTs and the green balloon.
I'm pedaling with all my might
(corporate as jihad)
right through your snakebitten chest.

NO BOTTLED WATER

I can't handle these harpsichordesque
"lived social spaces" where everything sounds like the word *esquire*

combined with "Qu'est-ce que c'est?" No, I much

prefer the radio-
active firs so blistered in Nasquitarkus, Maine that when the sea
exhales sodium, it can only make the feet

more painful in your attempts to tap to Dvorak's
Prague Waltz. Guess I'm partial
to Dionysus who resuscitates near-dead cardiac tissue, the almost hit

rearview wolf in the road on your way to Anchorage, lobster
boiled richer than rose in Atlantic waters, the good nauseousness

of brushed nipples. I can't cope
with the cadaver of rooms. Give me roe before

it's caviar. No Pellegrino, I'll risk Guardia with my sip if it
means I'll never have to stay put.

And if I tear off the violet watercolor wallpaper
of the cerebellum and write
a list of differences on the back, it will read as follows:

"While his eyes are a baked brown hue, stones deformed
by entropic piles of material, yours

are tide pools against a twisted schist landscape that
suck in herds of gorgeous elk, carnivorous plants, an in-

verse Papua New Guinea where exotic flowers bloom"
and it feels good to both of us that I can rip them off.

ONE BILLION AND ONE. MY NEW FAVORITE NUMBER.

I live in a boxcar
where Mission street is a
rotting bag of McDonald's

where the Rin Tin Tins
lick and lick
the saccharin off
envelopes of the blue/black sky

and Randy leaves another glass
with a purple scab of wine
outside my bedroom door while

I am fucking Dave because...
you never wash your dishes.

Depraved as a gypsy lineage
and anxious as *you're late for work*

again I work up a sweat
running toward the overturned train

where I spend most of my time
gathering the tin cans
of this upstanding gentleman's

nourishment. Nothing is what
I mean by the boxcar or

meant it to be. The moon has
her little ways, so why can't I?

Because the moon
is the oval-shaped white spot

of thick o fog
where I pull out my hairs
and steer another bad weather
day into the flesh.

BACKYARD STORY

Lungbasin of dirt–
water where

a rag wrung dry
of words was left

in the mouth of a girl with
insect yellow eyes:

a danger zone
an orange cone oh

to swerve down that bad–
boy alleyway again

where you spit
in my eye and I fucked you

until Santa Monica Blvd
bent its sunset

back into its chest,
where my body fit

into a clawfoot tub
of hair shavings

and fluids and now I sit
in my suburban suit

on this pharmaceutical
afternoon of no–

where longing
for the noose

I once was and
the tree branch.

HE PROMISED GREATER ADVENTURES IN NORTHERN FLORIDA

under a black bed linen he nicknamed "morgue breath,"
wore a necklace of Xanax, asked to borrow

my favorite lipstick and $200
for a rendezvous with his papa whom he fed pear soup

through a feeding tube I called "Old Saint Nick."
Whatever plan he had for botanizing the black gums,

the titi and the small-fluted papaw dissolved late one
night in his reminiscence of younger women

and when I pleaded, "Leader of the Slavic Languages
Department, won't you at least go to Albertsons with me?"

he replied, "The footpath from the north unit's picnic area
leads to Lemon Hole, one of the park's favorite snorkeling spots."

Men named Marvin sent him packages of exotic fruits with pre-
stamped return envelopes wherein he emptied the contents

on a trampoline specifically reserved for his papa's
exercise regime. I read books he wrote on the mysterious

bacteria affecting the taste of Apalachicola oysters
while he took naps in the refrigerator. When did I realize

I was closer to his dog, Pedro, than I would ever be to him?
One July evening—sky the color of a peacock feather—

he passed out on a Lake Ella park bench so I took Pedro, the out-
going tide of the Waccassa Bay. Never before had I been

so within this in-ness, so close to the ribbon hiss,
hot wind, pulsing through the arterial, arrow point of abandon.

who wanted to be Garson.
Garson was the boss. Not as if Garson's

going to buy you lox with those
bagels! So bad he stole Garson's

tux and wore it when he mowed
the lawn. There's Garson now beyond

the river there's a school of
salmon swimming through the temples.

So, what was Garson like when
he wasn't drinking he was a big shot

attorney who dated a journalist who
lived in Houston and had red hair

the color of cooked salmon. So bad
he stole his car when Garson was

out of town he took it to the
peepshow methinks it was a Corvette

and inside an overweight hooker pulling
duct tape off of her burnt inner

thigh, the rubber scent
of tires in the background. I'm tired

of this job. Garson's a liar and no one
believes his autistic son claims full custody

of said nervous tic. But the man who wants
to be Garson is no idiot and when I bend down

to pick up the scotch tape he stares
in my face, pyrotechnic goes the gaze, saying
you know you always wanted to be Garson.

BEWITCHING MY HOWDY IN EROS WEEDS,
I THOUGHT I'D REPLY FROM THE BARRACKS.

Ladies and Gentleman:

If I may yoke this folksong on a green hill into forensic evidence
or finance a mule to part the truth from   false bedrock
   you mustn't interrupt
            when a neuron herd   scatters the horizon clips
   the sound of antlers and hooves   is an angular rain:

You see the story of Daniel and Aaron   is Song of Solomon old
   on circus stilts. And while my atmosphere collected
rare cloud formations they
            burnished their disappointments,
wept on crosses if this was later in history—
   these fixed conquistadors of the Dog Star.

"Well put" was how Aaron reasoned about my writing—
"her hands are the gendarme if this is sightseeing,"
            [inconclusive]
   "her skin   is soft clam meat which should be
interpreted as   wanting to terrorize
            anyone   in her pinpoint company."

That I may submit something ritualistic as Grand Canyon light
bouncing   inside a porcelain vase   for the next exhibit?

Dan reasoned in an antiseptic cube
   which consisted of a field of ordinary buttercups or
   an anapestic ointment
            on a coast that was sinking, on a plate
tectonic that was crushing under, Chris,
         who became the new geology.
   But he read me
   all wrong—*starfish collector?   a woman of the arts and
crafts movement?   an admirer of dolphin song?*

IS YOUR NAME CONRAD?

Ire is Ichabod Crane's underwater *por favor*
or the Weimaraner breeder's
no dumb luck with these zygotes
and Rumpelstiltskin
in those "you're a big boy" pajamas
storming around the oak stump
chanting "what's my
name? what's my name?"

Fahrenheit's a Russian pogrom
(on said soma) or the archangel
of *really bad* credit card debt—milk stains
folded into bills where payoff's an aqueduct
rate (for 4 breasts).

Many a poltergeist did roam the core
of her busybody self and she dired him
right down to the belly button before
she swore him off against a crescent moon of
"beware your first born" trapped in a dungeon
pressing on secret stones or blackbird
singing in the dead
of night's agony of funk—

No, more like which bloodborne disease
would the mosquito
squeeze into his proboscis unto the skin dips a
quill methinks to ink.

I'll admit...it isn't for me.
Not anymore. Gluey
Septembers in the infidel's crotch, moistures
spiked with influenza
along the handles of the other
gal's expensive purse, the brouhaha
of "whir, whir, whir, the wheel went" under
the shivering fuchsias of Quasar B.

BLOWING KISSES FROM AN UNDERWATER CAVE

If flesh should be wholesome
like a fresh Washington apple then
I'm the malnourished flesh holes

thrown in a brown bag of joints
and I won't stop at stop signs or quit
the gamble when I'm obviously ahead.

When the oreganos of a Thursday morning
shift their aromas into my drugstore sleep, I feed

(in true parasitic fashion) on the blue meats
and yellow fats of your bully: the Law

of Osmosis. Pigeonholed as a halo of cells
around a pupil or growing outward like a green mold,

I declare all my bad behaviors to be an act
the way a kleptomaniac really wants

the attention of her father who is out snorkeling
with his latest girlfriend amongst those Bora Bora fish.

The tropical fish may swish their asses but they
batter the bloated hands that feed them

with their rainbow lips submerged and retarded.

RANSOM NOTE ATTACHED TO WOLF'S EAR

I lived alone. Poured

confetti through a sieve, ate lint
from an empty tin can of chickpeas.

Gibbons sneezed
moonrise from their white nostrils
and breaking a chandelier, into teardrop rosary beads hacked lockjaws
        tighter than tetanus,
sharper than a cactus plant
    where grating a greeting like you're
the welcome mat.

I lived in the wake
of Boomtown *Plus or Minus Stardom*
      that downed smaller jets with my jellyfish consistency,
         under a tarp I lived
      butta bread and butter wiser than aquamarine air currents, looser
        than the plucked skin on a chicken thigh.

I lived as an ornate
    red mold, spiraling molten from
  the contorted torso of an acrobat, in the hemlock's
      prick, in the *ergo,*
      anemone's purple arm wand waving
au revoir to the shut-up ships of cargo moving west to shore up
    their bright goods.

And otherwise ousted from "You, shut up."
      Spatula to sprinkled donut, from spork to the milk
        inside a shook coconut
    into Earth's anonymous G-force—textured like
    corpse fifty-six coughed
out of a newly named Way,

all the vortex neurons poured through
a diamond-shaped keyhole, the back door
of black shards bleed black light.

STEAM

THE AMERICA YOU LEARN FROM
(A POEM FOR GROCERY WORKERS)

Walking past the "we've got the power workers,"
    I say to myself "Metropolis, I'm back"
      with my stash of handkerchiefs, magician's top hat,
      stick-it-to-the-man smirk, picket sign
          between incisors, half-synthetic laugh, mouth full of false
starts, I kick around some ash-blue sparks pull my forehead into zigzags
        of cracked cement and then I do a jig
            on the electric grid, I do a jig
               in vermillion heels, my wool scarf woven
    from the citric acid saliva of stray dogs.

That the police cracked my arm in half? But I'm the King
of Cuffs, suspended in a three-minute breath hold
straightjacket from the San Francisco Bay—I pull dredged
    rabbit fat, my own appendix
from an underwater cave of leopard sharks and when my jellyfish brain
undulates, I regurgitate
    the keys to unwind these chains.

              ★

      Enough!
    What am I talking about? I have no house.
      I am entirely minimum wage. I am one
hundred percent punch in
    and out, sandbags under the eyes
    live from cage to cage—the ocean tides wet my
      dog leash long esophagus
    hooked to the neck of the moon howls
    hey Missy England, it's all the rage and
      —*thumbs up, Abu Gharib*

I am the lapse. The collapsed
left lung of a little boy
who would die before
the next administration
of fluids and electrolytes.
His name was Chris West
and in that lung was a squashed
ballad "down by the Bay
where the watermelons
grow" and oh
how blonde were
the hairs on his head and oh
how blonde were
his lucky-you hands.

No.
I am the stone
testicle, the arterial
ride on the roller coaster
that plummets
the stomach.
I'm the (now vegetable oil) Hummer
of Arnold Schwarzenegger
riding through
Beverly Hills and
everyone looks at me
so look at me you
palm tree bitch.

No, I'm not.
I am poor.
I am so poor
that I vomit pennies.
Dimes trash
the sunset

so count them
if you want to be
loved tonight.
In this economy,
I'm nothing,
my friends are nothing,
the poems that they write
are good for nothing
and there's nothing
they can do about it.
My good for nothing
friends steal meat
from the butcher
and then cut off
their fingers and feed
them to their cats—
those ethical monks.

The suffocation cats
enter your room
when you least expect it.
You cough blood because
you can't pay for
the doctor and fur
is clumping up in
your aorta again.
You buy those dime store
drugs—purple syrups,
red pills and wait under
a thin sheet of glass.

PONCE DE LEÓN AS FLORIDAPHILE

1.

longs for his mama
  in Spain eating red dirt because
that's what you're supposed to do when you want
  your son to make the new world embryo
   and bring it back in the form of
  "contemplating the object."

  Longs for the haunted house of the west, the
movement of minnows around his bull man torso
  when he is in the spring
   no one can see the lower half of his body—*perhaps*
  he has hooves?—beneath the
  surface a manatee's big toe
recounts her startling transformation from elephant
to "dweller of aquatic regions in Florida
  sometimes crushed in water control structures."

  Navigation locks, floodgates—what ever happened
to Mama? She died a long time ago
  a voice says "and now *he's eating dirt,*" because
  we all want to change.

2.

  Bubbles. The sky is the metallic dream
of *you're an alchemist all right.* His cold sweat dislodges
  the humors from their usual points on the compass rose.
He's going to have to try harder to find where rhizomes meet
  mice turn to glass, pass
the nuclear age with her slither hair
  turns the mirror
  white and howling, burns
   the size of dustbins.

3.

           Smoke off the Gulf spins
counterclockwise. Berserk compass. *I dream of the*
                code of the west. Just to hum a tomb,
       come up with another feat to turn this
       limestone to snowy fingerprints. And the sea,
            with her ten feet of froth
               when it hurricanes the fountain of youth
and you've found it here, adventurer, reckless boat
             modeled to fit the flesh, outfitted
with oxygen and a good book on the history of salt.

A SYSTEM OF SUFFICIENT COMPLEXITY

For Andrew Joron

is pleasant at midnight if you are in Marseille on a boat heading
to Africa, but unpleasant if you are before me, the way RNA, single-stranded
dwindles to geriatric loops
around our wrists
making bracelets of
mutating barnacles
on a red tide
toward Red Hill
wherein a wave
goes galactic down crushed
by other revolving waters
in sea mucus experiments.

Researchers at the Rand Corporation
held a dozen seagulls in their intent: nonlinear, ambiguous

their squawks were still theirs   on the air swarm above
there was a convection from a storm
much like the "Battle of Seattle" cages that equal the dominant ideology
or to grow planks
unable to change   to drift   the way wood does,
force with which
we garner inflection
and hold a shell to a mirror   makes the blood-marrow

ashamed of its softness, the animal who left it

so long ago, that salt thing—whistles wind in between cage bars
cannot saw their beaks off   with light.

The other she is a network of carved calcium, the "self-
organized heterogeneity" of that boat
she called herself whitewashed   in the "brief chance of snow"

when it falls inconsequentially inside
bubbling sea foam—or is this the romance

of human agency? harnessed by brief technicians
      of the iris, a world system   metastasizing
          in a think tank   boxed-in with recurrent zeros.

Animal hires her deathbed pyre of pine needles
adjacent to a plague that reads: *Here stood
the Giant Redwood, Bianca.*

We crossed the Bering Strait for this in an orange
gardening clog; we ate ammonia fish and cooked
them in our chloride song. She quivers long.

Her eyes, Nile long, drive the dolly into the next
blue screen century. What's next, century?
Give it to me. I am ready to climb your Rockies,

to wrap the Vitamin A liver in aluminum foil
and wear the snow paw of the polar bear
so no one else can touch it.

Pass the torch, passport. Add some chlorophyll
to your green card and then mix your back-
ward backbone with Miracle Grow.

These are the best seats I could find.
Here stands the auditorium of the "I," drinking
ice melt from a canister of film.

My name is scrotum, rice paddy,
Madonna, Windex, tampon, Camp
Electric Barb, and I have
a hardhat made of jelly,
crampons welded to my gums.

YOU SHOULD PUT A NEIGHBORHOOD ON THAT

Sit still, cosmos.
Attend to me.

There is teaching
and the taut. Do tell
where you were schooled.
Each silk orchid wows
they look so real
on my coffee table
oozing clear ozone
off their labellums.

I pass the days in black
and white filming a still life:
glass of carbonate beyond
the orchid reels soot
turned the moths
Darwinian logic.

Drink until you're full.

You're the way of the birds
that fuzz the sky's orange feathers.
Their morning calls
were on the posters
in my high school's computer lab
(the corporation bought them all)
and now their rodent
nibbled wires, buttermilk paint
over cinderblock walls
makes a campaign get to work.
A crumb for you,
and one for that kid
isn't me any more.

I've learned the way
of the crosswalk, and Fran
(the guard) who
held the DO NOT CROSS sign.
Her face went puce, her webbed
feet never did finish
her floral cross-stitch on which

she sets the breakfast table
to the sound of hornets' acoustics
across from the plant pumps
so much Chevron fuel
that half the town
I fled, I fled, flowers
in false cuttings.

CROSSING OUT THE ALPS

He sketches the Milky Way with a rock on soil
to show me where it breaks the skin.
Come on skin.
You can do it. The rabbit's pulse
is right there behind her fur twitches ears.
Pussy. Baby. Prick.

I plant a garden to dignify life.
You need so much chicken shit
for the tomatoes, butternut squash,
all eyes and ears on the drowned polar bear,
the hippo boiled in its tank,
the last elephant carrying
Hannibal across Etrurian marsh.

He sketches the birdsong like dot-
dot-dash, to show me
the world I don't understand: a bride
on the gazebo who recites a recipe for hummus: mash
garbanzo beans for seven minutes
between stalks of wild onion
that spring *Thy coral reef* sing
Thy Easter Island stone. Thy Icelandic music.

I see a circle on a red background
it is the sum or an
inversion of
the picture I see
        a red
        cell that
        will become
        an organ with which to hold
        the body
        together—that
        supposition of frame,
junction of trouble
and the means
by which entrance
and escape go
hand and hand out
the doorframe of
goodbye.
        Suppose it is a vessel
        that I am
        pointing at
        or an illusionary hand
        that you are
        taking away or that the line
is not vein
and I am only a somewhere
that has walked
through the skeleton
of somewhere
slipping away.
        Of course I could say
        "There is a red circle outside the square,"
        remark that the pigeons
        look like washcloths

from this kitchen window
that you are in yourself
a goodbye and a greeting
(as description is half the handshake

      that the retina grips.)
      Therefore, I don't see the circle anymore.
      It's the framework,
      the awkward

stepping
from the rowboat to
the gravel pathway
until the checkered kitchen.
A portrait which
in any other instance

     would call the face
     a collection of blue
     descriptors
     and the hand that
     drains the eye

a syntax of
arbitrary motions.
But *suppose this is*
my incomplete picture—
a hand left open
to the weather
cannot be constructed
as disjunction

    No cannot say or see.

LET ME OUT

Two black spots rotate counter-clockwise on the Io moth
and likewise I am fifty percent mimicry
fifty percent this oyster watercolorist
adjacent to Woolf's lighthouse where her
double helix hairs grow into
a litmus test turns acid rouge cheeks.

Scrub the sandpit with bleach and call it "a percentage
of the ocean's smell," a self replicating wound the consistency
of an antibiotic ointment on the jellyfish sting,
a blue base that froths in a porcelain vase.

My gaze face splinters a light maze as
your cheeks pink wind. In Hegel's inversions all ones
are blacked out and stuffed with apples
so coax-howl, raise these semen ships (for hell).

If I were you, I'd tighten that Victorian corset grip
to the spine lest you move into the moth's
nada wink. Now it's backing out of said corner,
the sound of air rushing into the puncture where the rib
went right through skin. You're identical twin #6
to the imaginary number e, Great Chain of Being,
the black ground where a lung deflates light.

LINES TO DEMARCATE STATES AND MAPS

With an idea of spring in mind, the deer
zigzag from cliffs toward our iridescent streetlights.

A new sign says "Here is the future home
of Building X" and sitting in the grass, our terrier

runs to chase an olive-colored lizard who darts
towards the pond, under the live oak's vines, six

overturned turtle shells, hardened and stripped
of their flesh and still, we want to take them back

to the house and rinse them off—to save or just
to wonder how their desires met the pond,

how Building X will look when this grass,
these turtles, snakes, the deer are gone.

Stay a while and read to me. Does the serpent
ever sleep? What is her fiction underneath those eyes?

Will she dine on eggs or will she give up food,
resolve an anorexia of space?

What sheer egomania. Corridors of torn
prints that scrap the world to parenthesis.

But we are mammalian, not built but heaved into
hair and milk—mixing mustard gas with blood

we happenstance, plan, and think *perhaps* from
air to a concrete slab—there is no going back.

Wet slumped weeds, the deer recede
and our calloused hands divide the mind, irregular
as a tumor gone wild from one wilted cell.

TOKYO ELEGY FOR ZACH OVER OKONOMIYAKI

For Zackary Hanson (1969-2006)

They took all his books today, the Beckett
and the Joyce, scrubbed the rings

underneath his empty coffee cups, boxed
them up as if stains

were portable. Tokyo seems like an interesting place
to give up—to wave the white flag

from the tallest building, construct
a continent from that. My star-shaped earrings

whooshed the artificial air conditioning of the room
where synapses zing, zoom

and spring like kidney beans in a yellowing jar
of water without the flowers. I couldn't stay. His mother

couldn't draw a breath and now I know what "mother"
means: The child clings to her metallic nipple.

Today oak wide, I walked oak's breadth from here to
California (home) where the ocean gurgles, shore

ripples salt to skin. And how earth troubles!
The dead hiccup dirt and milk-white branches

only hurt the living so it's the inverse of the hiccup
after all and we just stare motionless like the tree.

The mother will fly back to wherever she's from—Minnesota
or out west where there will be something short

of words to cradle the tongue where language
retrieves its deflated lungs. But what they

didn't find. He had a cutout of Beckett
on the file cabinet with a handwritten quote I couldn't bring

myself to read. I think of Bangladesh or Caracas
where fistfuls of babies are born of seed each instant,

mothers heavy with unfolding maps inside their blackened pupils,
and in one zap, that backward leap of the irretrievable,

the star planted in Voltaire's garden grows
or dies unbroken within or out its blue surroundings.

DEAR MONTANA,

For Zach Barocas

There is no g(ah-hum)d—.
Of that, I can be sure
and in going to Istanbul, well, that's when we notice the leather tower
    of Pisa, and it brings
us back to 9th grade mathematics; we notice
the soft glands on the red fish.

[Example: electron   selectron
                   photon   photino
                   gluon   gluino
                   graviton   gravition]

Youth's hopeful in its animal is.

But whatever gravitation blurred your woods—whatever weak pull
took
took such that it was impossible to stay alive.

The wilderness shook a bit
around the wrist, sucked in the trees as if

that green was born black as an embryo.

Splotch on the map.
New York. Los Angeles. Caracas. Baracas.

      Timber goes creek and we
      we walk in a figure eight.

TOMORROW'S BRIGHT BRACELETS

Winter lungs are white trees.
Winter lungs are bare white trees.
There are no ornaments because this isn't Christmas.

Put a silver ribbon in your hair.
Put on all of your bright bracelets and walk out into the feathered snow.
My eyes are pale like a crust of ice over a long river.

What would the gift-givers say if they saw us now?
What will they tell the world?

And when you are home: Open
all of the windows in your small house—take off

all of your clothes, and then take off all of your underclothes
and watch your flushed cheek turn gray in a mirror.

NOTES

Parable That Takes Place in Little Nathaniel's Closet: After Sigmund Freud's essay "The Uncanny."

A Poem for David Schubert: The poem gets its rhythm and overall feel from Schubert's poem "The Visitor."

Writing My Bike in Circles around This Poem to Prove That I Persist: This poem owes something to Dickinson's "I held my life with both my hands / to prove that I was there."

Their Cats: This poem owes something to Fernando Pessoa; this poem is for David Lau.

Ponce de León as Floridaphile: The line "I dream of the code of the west" is from Ted Berrigan's *The Sonnets.*

Crossing Out the Alps: The hippo boiled in its tank alludes to the novel *And The Hippos Were Boiled in Their Tanks* by Jack Kerouac and William S. Burroughs.

Visual Field (Wittgenstein): Some of the lines in italics are from Wittgenstein.

Tomorrow's Bright Bracelets: The phrase "bright bracelets" alludes to John Donne's "The Relic."

ACKNOWLEDGMENTS

I would like to thank the editors of the following publications where these poems were published or will be published (some of them in different form).

Action Yes!: Writing My Bike around This Poem to Prove That I Persist
Abraham Lincoln: Ransom Note Attached to Wolf's Ear
Barrow Street: Let Me Out
Cake: Ode to the Adventure Writer
Cannibal: Is Your Name Conrad?
The Canary: One Billion and One. My New Favorite Number.
Coconut: Blowing Kisses from an Underwater Cave
Colorado Review: A Poem for David Schubert; Tomorrow's Bright Bracelets
Effing Magazine: I Serengeti You; Crossing Out the Alps
Fascicle: Knapsack of Ritz Crackers
Fence: I Don't Deserve Your Riesling
GutCult: Dear Montana,
Keep Going: Lines to Demarcate States and Maps; Tokyo Elegy for Zach over Okonomiyaki
La Fovea: Once I Worked with a Man
Lana Turner: The Physiological Infestation of the Leap That Looks Back
Lungfull: A System of Sufficient Complexity; The America You Learn From
New Orleans Review: Visual Field (Wittgenstein)
No Tell Motel: He Promised Greater Adventures in Northern Florida
Pool: Their Cats
Seneca Review: These Days Are Malthusian Footnotes
Third Coast: Ponce de León as Floridaphile
Tight: I Am Small
The Tiny: Salt Latitudes
Volt: The Truth about the Pills I Took; Bon Voyage; Backyard Story

Sandra Simonds is the author of several chapbooks including *Tomorrow's Bright Bracelets* (forthcoming, Kitchen Press), *The Pyrotechnics of Madame Trotter* (forthcoming, Coconut), *Bananas and Spiders* (forthcoming, H_NGM_N), *A Teeny Tiny Book of War* (Teeny Tiny, 2008), *The Humble Travelogues of Mr. Ian Worthington* (Cy Gist, 2007), and *The Tar Pit Diatoms* (Otoliths, 2006) as well as the founder of *Wildlife,* an experimental, handmade poetry magazine. She earned a BA in English and Psychology from UCLA and an MFA from the University of Montana. She is currently a PhD student in Creative Writing at Florida State University and keeps a blog at ssandrasimonds.blogspot.com.